I Am Brave
By Aaron Fields

Copyright © 2025 Aaron Fields. All rights reserved.

Published by The Write Perspective, LLC

All rights reserved. No part of this book shall be reproduced or transmitted in any form or by any means, electronic, mechanical, magnetic, photographic including photocopying, recording or by any information storage and retrieval system, without prior written permission of the publisher. No copyright liability is assumed with respect to the use of the information contained in this book. Even though every precaution has been taken in preparation for this book, the publisher/author assumes no responsibility for errors or omissions. Neither is any liability assumed for any damage that results from the use of the information in this book.

ISBN: 978-1-953962-48-5

Being brave doesn't mean you're never scared—it means you try anyway.

In I Am Brave, meet Leo, a kind and curious kid who learns to find courage in everyday moments—from saying hello to new friends to facing bedtime darkness and doctor visits.

This heartwarming story helps children understand that bravery comes in many shapes and sizes. Featuring diverse characters, gentle storytelling, and a special parent guide, this book is the perfect tool to help children build resilience and confidence—one brave moment at a time.

This is Leo.

Sometimes, Leo feels big and bold.

Other times… not so much.

But every day, Leo finds a little bit of brave.

At school, Leo met someone new.

His tummy felt funny.

He wanted to hide.

But he smiled and said, "Hi!"

That was brave.

Later, he saw the tall jungle gym.

It looked... really tall.

Leo's knees wobbled.

But he climbed one bar.

Then another.

That was brave too.

At home, the lights went out.

It was dark. Very dark.

Leo hugged his bear.

"I'm okay," he whispered.

He closed his eyes.

Brave again.

One day, Leo had to get a shot.

He didn't want to.

He held his bear tight.

He looked away.

Then... it was done.

Leo took a deep breath.

"I did it," he said.

That was brave.

Brave doesn't mean not scared.

It means you try anyway.

Leo still feels nervous sometimes.

But now, he knows...

He is brave.

And guess what?

You are too.

"Why BRAVE Matters"

Young children face big emotions every day—new people, loud noises, unfamiliar places. Learning to face fears builds confidence, resilience, and problem-solving skills.

Your child learns what bravery looks like from you and from characters like Leo. They don't need to be fearless—they just need to know it's okay to feel scared and try anyway.

Try These at Home:

Role-play "brave" situations with toys or puppets.

Tell your child about a time you were brave.

Celebrate small moments of courage, like trying a new food or saying "sorry."

www.ingramcontent.com/pod-product-compliance
Lightning Source LLC
Chambersburg PA
CBHW041633040426
42446CB00024B/3493